What If I'm

How to Overcome Homosexuality OCD and Regain Control of Your Life

Osvaldo Jimenez

Copyright 2019 Osvaldo Jimenez

All rights reserved.

Disclaimer

This publication is designed to provide accurate and authoritative information in regard to the subject matter covered. It is sold with the understanding that the publisher is not engaged in rendering psychological, financial, legal, or other professional services. If expert assistance is needed, the services of a competent professional should be sought.

Adherence to all applicable laws, including but not limited to international, federal, state, and local regulations governing professional licensing, business practices, advertising, and all other aspects of doing business in the United States or any other jurisdiction is the sole responsibility of the purchaser or reader.

Neither the author nor the publisher assumes any responsibility or liability on behalf of the purchaser or reader of the book.

Dedication

This book goes out to any adolescent out there who is scared and trying to find a way to help their condition. I've been there, and it was a terrible experience. This book is for you and all the people who have been afraid to share their deepest and most shameful secrets. You are not alone, and I can't wait to hear about every one of your incredible journeys.

Table of Contents

Disclaimer 3

Dedication 4

Introduction 7

What is OCD and Common Misconceptions about OCD ..11

Questions You Might Have 18

The Things You've Tried and Why They Didn't Work 26

Where it all started: Middle School 35

The High School Years 42

The College Years 48

Making the Decision to Finally Get Some Help. 53

How I Finally Learned to Manage My Thoughts. 60

What to Do When You Get an Unwanted Thought 68

Step by Step Guide on Tackling HOCD 75

Embrace Your Sexuality 94

Current Outlook on OCD 99

What to do if this book wasn't enough? 104

Can You Do Me A Favor? 107

About the author 108

Bibliography 109

Introduction

"Are you okay?" Is a question we get asked many times throughout our lives, and many times, we lie to avoid talking about our problems. I know this first hand because I lived through it, and to some extent, I still do it today. I'm sure many people prefer to keep their emotions hidden because they'd rather not bring out all their emotional baggage on someone just for asking a question. If you're reading this book, chances are, you're not okay at the moment, but that's fine.

I have been dealing with Homosexuality OCD since I was 12 years old. For many years, I grew up ashamed and scared of what was going on inside of me. It wasn't until recently that I found the courage to act and face my demons head-on. It wasn't easy writing a book that revealed my deepest and darkest secrets throughout my life, but it also felt good just to let it all out there. I've been mulling over the idea of writing a book that discusses my form of OCD for a while but was hesitant from my inexperience as an author and general writer. I thought to myself, "If it helps people, then I should do it!" I'm glad that you have decided to take a step in the right direction in realizing that you also need help.

If there's one thing I know, is that people who deal with HOCD do not want to tell anyone about what's manifesting inside their head. You're probably reading this book in secrecy as you don't want people to be shocked that you're reading something with the title, *What If I'm Gay?* On the cover. I get that, and that's completely fine. You're not ready to be open about it yet, and more importantly, you're scared. The thing is, I understand where you're coming from because I was there. I would eat dinner with my family, and then go straight to my room and look up articles on the internet that contained any information about HOCD. I would pretend to be happy when I wasn't.

Trust me; I was there through it all. The panic attacks, constant checking for reassurance, wondering If I found my male friends attractive, questioning my attraction to women, and avoiding numerous encounters with people. This book will serve as a guide, as a mentor, and an inspiration for you anytime you feel like you can't pull through.

Trust me, you can, and you will. I believe in you.

For a precise definition, Homosexuality OCD is a subset of OCD in which sufferers constantly question their sexuality. They perform hidden mental compulsions to try to counteract their unwanted thoughts.[1] Common compulsions include:

Avoidance.
You stop dating, attending events, or going out into social settings.
Checking.

---

[1] Intrusive Thoughts. "Sexual Orientation OCD." *Intrusive Thoughts*, www.intrusivethoughts.org/ocd-symptoms/sexual-orientation-ocd/.

Looking at someone or a picture of someone of the same sex and determining whether you have a sexual or emotional response.

Questioning.
Becoming confused when you see someone of the same sex and thinking they're attractive.

Reassurance.
Looking at photos or porn of the opposite sex to confirm that your sexual desires are aligned with what you know to be true.

When I first started having unwanted thoughts about my sexuality, I felt like the world was crashing down on me. I didn't know what to make of it, nor did I know what to do. There wasn't much I could find at the time regarding my unwanted thoughts. I searched through the web for hours when I got home from school and was always disappointed when I found nothing that could help me out.

It was a scary time filled with anxiety, panic attacks, and isolation. It took me ten years to figure out how to control and manage my intrusive thoughts. It wasn't easy by any means, but it can be possible with the right treatment and guidance. Don't worry; it won't take you ten years to overcome HOCD. That's the whole reason you bought this book because you're tired of questioning your sexuality and you want to live your life stress-free. I hope by reading this book, you can relate your own experiences in some way and find helpful tips on beating your HOCD.

This book is designed for anyone dealing with unwanted and intrusive thoughts regarding their sexuality. I don't care if you're thirteen or fifty-five; this book can help you in ways that I wished it could've helped me when I was younger. This book is a compilation of advice that I have received from months of therapy, books, and general knowledge from others who are suffering from this anxiety disorder.

First, we need to kill some common misconceptions about HOCD that you've probably heard before.

What is OCD and Common Misconceptions about OCD

Ask your friends or family to define OCD, and I'm sure they'll give you the typical answers many people have in their head. They'll probably say it involves germaphobes who have to wash their hands all the time or people who have to check the stove two to five times before they go to bed. People tend to think that OCD is visible when that isn't always the case.

I remember discussing my OCD for the first time with a friend of mine in our college library. My friend brought a partner along with him because they were working on a project, and he overheard our conversation.

"You have OCD? But you look normal?" Is what he told me. I wasn't offended, nor did I care about the comment, but it did make me realize how misconstrued OCD is for many people. For a long time, I thought the same thing as well. I used to believe that someone had to show signs that they had a mental illness or else, I would assume they were doing ok. Later in life, I realized that many people are capable of putting on a friendly smiling face while they're hurting deep down. It's a sad reality for many people, and we go through life not knowing how people are feeling most of the time.

If you remember from the introduction, I gave you a definition for HOCD, but need to inform you about POCD as well.

Purely Obsessional OCD is a form of OCD in which a person has unwanted and intrusive thoughts, **but** instead of having physical compulsions as some OCD sufferers do, they perform hidden mental compulsions.[2] Usually, people who have POCD suffer from violent, sexual, and other types of unwanted thoughts. So, people often put the first letter of the word that describes their intrusive kind of thought.

For example:
1. People who have unwanted and sexual thoughts about children have Pedophilia OCD
2. People who have unwanted thoughts about their sexuality have Homosexuality OCD, which is what this book is about.
3. People who have unwanted thoughts about suicide have Suicidal OCD.

It is a commonly accepted practice for many people to categorize their OCD this way as it helps them identify it.

Purely Obsessional OCD is a term that was developed by Dr. Steven Phillipson. He created this term when he started receiving patients who felt like they had OCD but didn't engage in the physical compulsions that many people associate with OCD. He noticed that they had intrusive thoughts that would cause them great distress, but their compulsions involved rituals and were more

---

[2] Intrusive Thoughts. "Pure OCD." *Intrusive Thoughts*, www.intrusivethoughts.org/ocd-symptoms/pure-ocd/.

discreet. Dr. Phillipson said that the technical term is non-observable ritualizers, but his patients preferred the term Pure OCD because it was much easier to say, and they liked having a term that distinguished them from the common form of OCD.

Since Pure OCD is a nickname for a type of OCD, medical professionals don't diagnose people with it. This tends to be harmful to many patients because they end up going to therapists or specialists, who are not educated in the type of treatment they need. In my case, I went to see a counselor in college about my intrusive thoughts, but it was a counterproductive session because she gave me useless advice and didn't know how to diagnose me. There's more on that experience later in the book.

Many people who deal with Pure OCD, don't seek treatment or tell anyone about their condition. They're overwhelmed with fear and anxiety about how they'll be perceived if they do speak out, so they decide to keep it hidden. I did that for many years, and it was hell. Don't make that same mistake in making it seem like your life is filled with nothing but happy thoughts when it's not.

Here's a list of common misconceptions people have about OCD.

1. **There's no such thing as HOCD (Homosexual OCD)**.
   Fact: People with OCD obsess over a lot of things, and one of those things is their sexuality. If you're

dealing with HOCD, then there's a high chance that you've thought about HOCD not being a real thing and that you might be gay. I thought the same thing for an extended period until I did further research and concluded that it is a real thing. Many respected psychiatrists, like Dr. Steven Phillipson, have come out and talked about the validity of HOCD while giving common symptoms, treatment options, and background information.

I understand that HOCD is not categorized in the DSM, this is a handbook that medical professionals use for diagnosing mental disorders, but just because the DSM doesn't have a specific term listed doesn't mean that it can't be added later. The DSM is continually being updated with new information, and at one point, believe it or not, had homosexuality categorized as a mental disorder. Take that HOCD skeptic!

2. **People with OCD are super neat-freaks.**
   Fact: This couldn't be further from the truth, and I'll explain why. Many people who suffer from OCD don't even associate themselves with being neat-freaks. Yes, there are some sufferers of OCD who have fears of being contaminated with germs or dirt. Those people tend to wash their hands or clean appliances religiously, but some only experience unwanted thoughts about harm, religion, etc. OCD is a complex anxiety disorder that doesn't fall into one category, and not everyone suffers the same symptoms.

3. **OCD requires physical compulsions.**
   Fact: Washing hands, flicking the light switch, or tapping something repeatedly are all common images people get when OCD is discussed. The truth is that OCD is a complex mental illness that affects many people who suffer from it differently. Many sufferers go through hidden mental compulsions like checking, praying, performing rituals, and avoiding certain circumstances. Usually, people who suffer from POCD have mental compulsions that go unnoticed and can be more tricky to diagnose.

4. **Subconsciously, this is what you want and who you are.**
   Fact: One of the biggest lies we are told is that our inner thoughts represent the dark side of our personality; that is actually who we are as people. That couldn't be further from the truth since many people tend to have weird and arbitrary thoughts all the time. As an example, let's say that you went downstairs to eat something. You decided to make a sandwich, and while you're putting it together, you thought of what would happen if you started smearing mayonnaise all over your arm. It's a random thought that came to your head, but it doesn't mean you're going to do it.

   Suffering from Pure-OCD; however, means that you cannot make this distinction. Others would react to intrusive thoughts with indifference because of their appropriate relationship with their thoughts. If you suffer from Pure-OCD though, pervasive anxiety ensues these kinds of images that make you unable to let them go. You need to learn that your thoughts have nothing to do with who you are as a person. The way you live your life and the choices you make are what truly represent your character.

Usually, people with POCD have violent and sexual thoughts that they want to get rid of, and they start to believe that these thoughts could mean that they subconsciously want to do these horrific things. They feel like they're bad people for having these thoughts and will beat themselves up about it since they feel like they shouldn't even be thinking about it.

Nothing is wrong with you, and you just have a hard time letting those thoughts be what they are, just thoughts.

There's a big chance that if you're reading this book, you've probably put on a happy mask for people to see when in reality, you might have been in a dark place mentally. It's human nature for people to hide their emotions and not want to cause a spectacle about what's going on in their lives. There has to be a point in which we have to admit to ourselves that it's ok to talk about what's going on in our lives and break the stigma surrounding Homosexuality OCD.

Questions You Might Have

1. **Is it gay to notice if another man is attractive?**
   No, no, no, and no. Did I say no enough times yet? Since you have HOCD, you're more susceptible to thinking there's more to thought than there is. Growing up, I used to think that all straight guys never noticed if another man was good looking let alone admit it in public. As I grew older and saw what was happening in my surrounding environment, I realized how ridiculous that was. I have no problem admitting if someone is handsome and you shouldn't be either. We're not saying we want to have sex with them, nor that we want to be in a relationship with them, it's just truthful.

   Look at how girls describe each other; they always give each other compliments, hold hands, and throw heart eyes at each other through social media any chance they get. I'm not saying to smack your buddy's ass or say, "bitch, you look amazing!" Just be confident in yourself to realize that it doesn't make you gay to notice obvious things.

2. **What makes you an expert?**
   What makes an "expert" anyway? Is it years of experience, or having a fancy title that you can put up on your wall? There are plenty of licensed or certified therapists and psychologists who don't know how to deal with people with Pure OCD.

Some of the worst advice I ever received was from a licensed school counselor who had a degree in psychology. I've been exactly where you have been: scared, alone, and anxious.

Having this type of mental illness isn't a gift you want to have, but I was blessed with the knowledge and tips that I was able to use in helping to control my Homosexuality OCD. I don't have a Ph.D. nor do I have a degree in psychology, even though I probably know more about OCD through books than some person with a general Psychology degree, but that's beside the point. I've lived through this, and you don't need a title to give some quality advice. All you need is experience and desire to help others who have faced the same obstacles you have.

3. What should I do if I relapse?

There's always going to be a chance of relapse, and you shouldn't fear it. Take it as a chance to show you off your new techniques against these thoughts. Relapse is a term used to describe people who get better at managing their thoughts but eventually regress to their old mindset. This hasn't happened to me, and I hope it doesn't happen to you. There could be a possibility of relapse for some, but you'll have this book for guidance in case you do regress.

You'll learn how to live with these thoughts with specific techniques discussed later in the book, but don't worry if you find yourself giving up. Getting better at handling these thoughts took me months, and it wasn't easy. I still deal with these kinds of thoughts, but I'm much better at managing them.

4. **Sometimes, I feel like I'm getting an impulse to do something sexual with the same sex. Why?**
What if I told you that impulses are just illusions? If you didn't get that Morpheus reference, then there's no hope for you. I'm kidding about that Morpheus reference. It turns out; you're experiencing *anxious thinking* when you're feeling like you have to put in a lot of effort to not act on what you're thinking about. According to psychologists, anxious thinking is an altered state of awareness, and it causes your perception to change drastically.

Psychologists have coined the term *thought-action fusion*, which happens when the line between thoughts and actions becomes fuzzy and unclear. Thoughts and actions are entirely different things, but when one is anxious, the difference seems to fade away. So, when you're trying hard to avoid a thought, your anxiety will go through the roof, causing your perception between thoughts and actions to dwindle. So, even though it might feel like you're having all these sexual impulses, it's your perception of thoughts and actions that's been distorted.[3]

---

[3] Winston, Sally, and Martin N Seif. "Overcoming Unwanted Intrusive

From my personal experiences, being near certain guys was tough. I remember when I was in college, I would hope that there wouldn't be any good-looking guys in jobs that I worked at. If there were, I would immediately get anxious and would start to think that I was going to find them attractive, so that made things uncomfortable for me. Seriously, my brain made things hell for me sometimes because there would be certain guys that many people wouldn't consider attractive, but I would still find myself getting scared to be around them in fear of thinking I would later find them attractive. People with HOCD know about that annoying little voice in the back of their head that keeps instigating their thoughts and makes it seem like you want to act on those thoughts.

5. **I had a stimulating groinal response to a gay sex scene! Does that mean I'm gay!**
Ok, now let's calm down and breathe slow. Did you do it yet? Alright, let's untangle this taboo subject together. Sex is a complicated thing, and under the right circumstances, sexual things of any kind can cause arousal for anyone. Have you ever seen two animals having sex or performing sexual acts on each other? Well, there's a good chance you might have found that sexually stimulating, even though

---

Thoughts." *NewHarbinger.com*, New Harbinger Publications, 25 Aug. 2019, www.newharbinger.com/overcoming-unwanted-intrusive-thoughts.

you're not attracted to animals. Dr, Fred Penzel, a psychologist, talked about this extensively about how he had patients who talked about getting sexual feelings from things that are considered taboo or looked down upon. Usually, these things included incest, pedophilia, and same-sex porn.

I remember testing myself out by watching gay porn to see if it would cause any pleasurable sensations for me. Having some stimulation doesn't make you attracted towards the same sex. So, remember, it's very common for many people to find certain taboo subjects on sex that they find stimulating, but would never actually engage in.

6. **What's wrong with me and will I ever get better?**
I remember asking myself this question all the time to the point where I contemplated suicide. I knew I never was going to kill myself, but there were times where it felt like being dead would be better off than living a life with a fake smile, and pretending everything was ok. I am here to tell you that it can get better. With the right techniques and with some motivations, your recovery is limitless. It's all up to you to push yourself to get better and handle this.

Let's get something straight. Nothing is wrong with you. You have thoughts that many people have as well. The only difference is that your approach to thoughts is what causes anxiety and confusion.

People like you and I don't let thoughts just be thoughts, and that's where we can improve on and get better.

7. **Where do these thoughts come from?**
That's a question we all want to know. Well, thankfully, we know some of the science behind intrusive thoughts, and thanks to Dr. Steve Phillipson. According to Phillipson, it's not completely clear how Intrusive thoughts are caused, but it could be due to misfired signals in the amygdala. The **amygdala** is the part of your brain that is responsible for detecting fear and preparing for emergency events. So, when amygdala comes up, your first thought should be fear.

According to Dr. Phillipson, the amygdala is a portion of the brain that has a malfunctional misfiring mechanism that causes the brain to associate fear with your intrusive thoughts because it doesn't like to feel fear without an association. This creates an authentic experience of fear with your thoughts, even though they are just meaningless thoughts.

It's no secret that these thoughts scare us. What do we want to do with things that we're afraid of? We want to get rid of them as soon as possible, and the sooner we figure out how, the better. That's why the amygdala is critical here because it represents fear, and it creates a false sense of danger with these thoughts.

That's how we feel about these thoughts. It freaks us out that there could be a possibility of us liking people from the same sex, especially when it relates to close friends and other acquaintances.

8. **Why does it feel like I'm losing my attraction to the opposite sex?**
One of the reasons why many sufferers feel this way is because of all the anxiety and confusion HOCD has created in their mind. I'm sure before HOCD came into their life, they didn't think twice about being attracted to the opposite sex. They could look at a girl or guy and not have any what-if questions that made them doubt their undeniable attraction to them.

When the brain is filled with constant anxiety, this will trick and confuse sufferers to constantly overanalyze every attraction they experience. To give an example, I was helping this girl with her HOCD and she would tell me that every time she saw an attractive guy—she would say "He's cute," but would then get an unwanted thought like "You're just saying that because you don't want to admit you're gay."

She would tell me that this constant battle with her thoughts would cause her to consider if she was ever attracted to men and how she felt like she was losing her attraction as more unwanted thoughts came. She wasn't losing her attraction to men, but she felt this way because of the confusion her thoughts caused her.

You have to remember that HOCD will do everything in its power to get you to fuel it with constant compulsions. Don't let HOCD ruin your life by making you think that your undeniable attraction to the opposite sex is being taken away.

I hope that answered most of what was on your mind. Now, we will move on to the things you tried and why they didn't work.

Trust me. I know all too well about this process.

The Things You've Tried and Why They Didn't Work

There's a likely chance that you've already tried to get rid of these thoughts before, but you failed miserably. I know the feeling because I tried to do the same things you did. These thoughts felt like the worst thing imaginable, so I kept it hidden for years, and I thought I could handle it myself when that wasn't the case at all. If you're anything like me, which you probably are since you're reading this book, then you've probably practiced techniques that involved trying to ignore the thought, reassure yourself, and avoid things completely. We'll go over why these techniques didn't work, and how they make your condition worse.

1. **You tried to ignore the thought as much as you could.**
   Let's play a game where I tell you not to think about your grandma taking shots while smoking weed with a bunch of college kids at a party. Ok, go for it. I'm sure it'll be a piece of cake. **Wrong!** One of the essential things that I and many others who suffer from HOCD do is try to rid ourselves of a thought we don't like. Usually, it has little success since our brain works in mysterious ways.

   With HOCD, sufferers try hard to not think about their unwanted thoughts towards the same sex, but to no avail. You probably noticed that when you started getting some unwanted thoughts about the same sex, you immediately tried hard not to think about them. You tried to think of something else or tried to distract yourself by engaging in an activity. This probably made it worse or didn't help your condition at all.

Why this didn't work.
Like I stated in the previous paragraph, the brain works in mysterious ways. According to a psychologist, Daniel Wagner, trying hard not to think about something only guarantees that you **will** think about it. He is the author of the book, *White Bears and Other Unwanted Thoughts: Suppression, Obsession, and the Psychology of Mental Control,* and he describes how when people try not to think about a thought, the brain has two different parts working against each other. One part of the brain is searching for distractions, and the other part is monitoring to see if you're able to stop thinking about the thought, but this enhances the thought and makes it stay longer.

We are not going to be ignoring the thought. We will be doing the opposite, but we'll get to that later in the book.

2. You avoided a lot of situations.
Avoiding is never a good thing, not just in HOCD but in many aspects of life. When you avoid certain situations, you're putting off the fear of something that you'll eventually have to face. Avoiding people

and places only make your condition worse, because that shows that HOCD has gained control over your life.

When I first started dealing with HOCD, I avoided certain TV shows, movies, and topics of discussion. I was really into this show called *Teen Wolf* in my freshmen year of high school, but I later stopped watching it because I couldn't handle my unwanted thoughts. There were a lot of attractive people in that show, and by looking at some good-looking men, I felt anxious and worried all the time. When I was in school, I didn't want to be near some guys in the locker room because I felt like I might get turned on by seeing half-naked dudes all around me. I let HOCD dictate what I was able to enjoy and what my days would consist of. For a while, I truly felt like I was never going to enjoy the activities I participated in before HOCD came into my life. This didn't help me at all, and I was left living in a deprived social setting for a long time.

Why this didn't work
Avoiding things, in general, is not a good way to live by. Whether it's avoiding talking to a person you like, putting yourself out there, or telling people how you truly feel. When you avoid, it means that you can't fully live the life you truly want. It's the same concept with your unwanted thoughts because once you start avoiding certain places, people, or entertainment, you're letting your thoughts know that they have power over

you. This is destructive behavior, and it will do us no good here.

3. You kept trying to reassure yourself

"I can't be gay. I've never liked a guy in my life! Why is this happening to me?"

Sound familiar? I know it does for me and I'm sure for many of you reading this. For the longest time, my way of handling my thoughts was to try and reason with them. I knew my thoughts were crazy and illogical, so I always felt the need to rationalize in the hopes that I would feel better or cured. Reassurance can help at first because it seems like you've finally talked some sense into those stubborn unwanted thoughts, but that doesn't end up lasting.

According to Fred Penzel, some common ways sufferers look for reassurance when dealing with HOCD are:

- Looking at attractive men or women to see if they are sexually attracted to them.
- Masturbating or having sex repeatedly to check their reaction to it.
- Paying attention to how they walk, talk, and act to make sure they don't come off as gay.
- Looking back at their past and trying to remember how they acted or thought about straight or gay people.
- Checking people's reactions to see if they start noticing certain gay traits in oneself.

- Reading articles on how people know they are gay or straight. They will also read coming out stories to see if there is any resemblance to their own story.
- Constantly asking others or seeking reassurance about their sexuality.

Why didn't this work?
One of the reasons why reassurance doesn't work is because the doubt always comes back. When it does come back, it comes in full force, and it won't go away quickly. Let's say that you just finished calming down your HOCD by telling it that you've always had crushes on girls and that this doesn't make sense for these thoughts to come out all of a sudden. This calms you down, and you feel good. You're fine for five to ten minutes, but then you get an unwanted thought like, "What if being gay is who I truly am now, and this is actually what you want?"

Now, you have to find reassurance again from something else to rationalize this thought. You see how the cycle never ends, and it's just one big bundle of joy.

In this book, there's not going to be any ridiculous methods of reassurance, and you'll be better off without it.

4. Praying

When nothing else works, how about a quick praying session, am I right? Nothing seems more gratifying than to openly give yourself up to God and have him fix all your problems. The reality is that this tends to be disappointing on every level. One thing I don't want to do is downplay religion or discredit it on every platform, but it doesn't serve us any good here. I was there as well, on my knees and in my room begging for all this to stop. When nothing else seemed to work, I felt like I could count on praying to save me from my mind.

Why this didn't work
There is nothing wrong with praying, and I don't want you to think praying is useless. It can genuinely give comfort when needed. When it comes to helping your HOCD, well, that's a different story. The only person capable of doing that is yourself, and that's all you will need. When we pray, we are putting all the pressure of getting rid of our unwanted thoughts on an existential force. That's not how your brain will get rewired. Praying can make some people feel better, but it doesn't address factors like avoidance, reassurance, and contradictions you will feel consistently.

5. **You tested your groinal response by watching porn or other methods**
   This had to be one of the first things I did when I suffered from HOCD. I would watch straight porn, gay-porn, and lesbian porn to check which one would give my penis a more stimulating experience. I would do this for days each time I came home from school and would look at my penis and then check the screen and observe what would happen.

I hadn't yet discovered masturbating at this point in my life, so my tests would consist of checking to see if I had an erection to specific scenes. I found the straight and lesbian porn to be the most sexually stimulating, but I couldn't say the same thing about gay porn. I thought, "That settles it. I'm not gay!" Even though I was able to see that I had no interest in seeing two men participate in sexual activities, this did nothing to help me in the long run. I would still regularly check my reactions anywhere I could: at my school when I watched TV, and sometimes, I would daydream about being with a man.

Why this didn't work
Jon Hershfield, a psychotherapist, trained in OCD, explains that testing yourself by masturbating to various types of sexual acts is tricking your mind into thinking that you're performing exposure, but you're performing more compulsions. He describes this method as "a wolf in gay clothing." By continuously masturbating to different sexual themes, you create a cycle of conditioning yourself to be aroused by your fears, and that will only make matters worse.

Also, Hershfield states that constant masturbation can act as bait for your HOCD by continuously making you perform more compulsions. When you're testing yourself, the process becomes a chore because you start treating masturbation like a clinical study where you're constantly monitoring your reactions.

"Was my orgasm as big as it was for this scene as it was for the last one?" and "Was my penis that hard?" are some common questions that will arise when you're constantly testing yourself for hours and hours.

Not only does testing create more compulsions, but it serves as reassurance for your thoughts by keeping you stuck in a never-ending cycle of what-if questions. You'll end up with an enormous history of gay porn on your laptop and will be left with even more confusion than when you started!

Now that we got all that stuff out of the way, I need to brief you on my story. You might find some similarities in our stories, and for others, it might seem like you're reliving your childhood.

My HOCD story started when I was twelve years old and lasted up until I turned twenty-three years old. It was a long and tumultuous journey, but one of the significant benefits you'll receive from reading about my story is learning from my previous failures to address my condition, and how you can improve upon that.

It was hard to go back and write out some of my most private moments, but it was an essential thing to do and showed how much I've truly improved. One of the things I hope you take from my story is that the ability to get better is not impossible. It will be something you will accomplish, as well.

Where it all started: Middle School

My life has always been what many people consider "a normal childhood." Growing up, I played with friends from my neighborhood and thought about things that almost every kid thinks of: playing video games, and junk food. Looking back, it's easy to see why many people miss their childhood.

As we grow old, things change. We enter puberty and start to find things out about our body that never crossed our mind before. Life becomes more abstract and complicated.

The day my OCD came was one that I will never forget. I remember having that initial thought of "What if I'm gay?" and as the days progressed, it just got worse.

I was 12 years old in 7th grade, going into 8th. I used to watch a lot of MTV during that time, and there was this show called *The Real Word*. It was a show about getting a group of strangers and placing them into a house to see what would happen for several months. I watched that show early on in my adolescence and found it to be entertaining. I probably shouldn't have been watching it considering it was filled with sex scenes, curse words, and adult entertainment that wasn't meant for a kid of my age.

The season I was watching was called "The Real World: Denver." There was a contestant on the show called Davis, and he was openly gay. In one specific episode, he starts describing his story about how he grew up in a southern Christian family and playing numerous sports. You could say he was a popular kid who had a good upbringing. He talked about how he started questioning his sexuality when he was in the six grade, and eventually went to therapy over it. He ended up being gay and was evident by his countless sexual encounters with men throughout the season. I didn't think much of that when I was watching the show, but that didn't last for long.

Life was normal, but as the days progressed, I started asking myself, "That's pretty crazy, I wonder what would happen if I was gay?" One of the reasons I think the thought stuck with was the fact that I was in middle school, and Davis found out his sexuality in middle school. Everyone knows how middle school can be. That's usually the time where you're trying to find your style or struggling with being accepted by your peers. Middle school is usually the introduction to things like relationships, masturbation, changing bodies, and becoming a teenager. It's an exciting yet cringeworthy time all wrapped in one.

I still get sad when I think of this time in my life. This isn't something I would wish on any child nor any adult. These thoughts consumed my life, and nothing else seemed to matter.
I didn't know it yet, but this was the beginning of a decade long struggle with unwanted and intrusive thoughts

"Well, I am going through puberty, and this is the time where many people find out their sexuality, so could I? No way! You've always been attracted to girls and have a crush on someone right now.

My brain became a back and forth battle on trying to find out if I could turn out gay. Instead of spending my days after school playing video games and watching tv, my mind became obsessed with finding out if I could be gay or not.

After I started having these thoughts, nothing was the same anymore.

I couldn't look at certain guys anymore without thinking I was going to do something sexual with them. I couldn't look at TV shows anymore because I felt like I might find an actor attractive and I felt weird around some of my friends.

One time, I met this guy through my friend at his house, and we immediately hit it off, since we had a lot of things in common. We talked about girls, video games, and school — things all young boys have on their mind at that point. The next time I saw him was different, and I could sense it.

He was at my house with two of my other friends. I wasn't happy to see him, and I was scared of even being in the same room with him. The HOCD thought had taken over by this point, and I kept thinking, "What if I want to kiss him?" or what if I start having unwanted sexual thoughts about him even though I didn't find him attractive at all." I kept thinking, "This isn't who I am; why is this happening to me?"

As you could imagine, that night didn't go the way I would have liked. I was scared, anxious, and felt like I had impulses to do things I didn't want to do. It didn't stop there, and it only got worse.

When I would hang out with my friends at school, I would have sudden urges to yell, "Guys, I'm gay!" out of nowhere. This would cause me to have significant anxiety when I was in a big group of people where I would have to breathe in and out at a slower pace. Also, I was bombarded with intrusive thoughts like "Dude, you're gay. Stop denying it." It felt like someone had taken over my body and kept yelling things I didn't want to hear.

What came after this was constant reassurance from anything I could find. I started looking at porn to test myself, I would check my groin to see if I had any response to sex scenes in movies, and I would look at girls' bodies at school. I remember this specific instance where I was in science class, and this girls' boob accidentally got pushed up against where my hand was, and my penis shot up like a rock. I was ecstatic, to say the least, it felt like my problems were over. Oh, but I didn't realize that HOCD role another way and doesn't leave that quickly. Right after this happened, the thoughts were still there telling me that I was gay, and that moment meant nothing.

During this time, I would always have my guard up about "appearing gay" to the people around me. HOCD had me questioning my previous experiences with girls and guys. I started analyzing the girls I had crushes on, and then I would ask myself if I ever truly liked them. I would get so paranoid when one of my friends would make a joke about me being gay. Usually, this consisted of calling me a "faggot," or any other derogatory gay term. I would laugh and play along, but then I would ask questions like, "Why did he call me a faggot? Did I appear gay at the moment?" Every single thing that involved people making comments about my sexuality had to be analyzed and processed over and over again.

I remember this specific instance in my 7th-grade year that involved this girl I found very annoying. I was sitting on my assigned number in PE class, just waiting for the teacher to arrive. As I was sitting down and minding my own business, the girl comes up to me and says, "Hey, you're gay huh!" I looked at her with a confused look and told her, "No, I'm not." I knew she was trying to be annoying because she wouldn't drop the subject. She kept telling me that I was in the closet and that I should just come out already. I was getting annoyed at this point, and that's when I shouted at her, "Shut up fat-ass!".

Now, this girl was overweight, and I could tell that I hit a nerve when I said that. I didn't feel bad at the time because she wouldn't stop harassing me with false accusations about my character. Eventually, she stopped annoying me with her comments after I said that, and it didn't cross my mind until HOCD became prevalent in my life.

I would ask myself, "Why did she say that to me? Do I come off as gay?" I kept looking back at that moment and would start to think if it was something about my body language that made her say those comments about me. Now, I know that she was probably an annoying teenager who just wanted to pick on someone. However, that moment truly made me question if there was something about me that came off as homosexual.

I was in a constant search for the truth, and it would kill me if I didn't find out what I was. Was I straight or gay? I had to know, and I wouldn't stop until I knew. I would watch straight porn, and then look at gay porn and would test to see if I had a stronger reaction to either one.

This completely took over my life to the point where I couldn't sleep right. I went to bed with anxiety and constant fear of what people would think if they knew what was going on. At my middle school, I was constantly hearing anti-gay things from almost everyone. "That's so gay," and "What a Faggot" were things I heard consistently. I would laugh, but inside, I was feeling miserable. Not only was gay looked at as a bad thing, but it made me feel like I couldn't express my concerns with anyone, and that only made it worse.

When I would eat dinner with my family, I just thought about what would my parents think if I told them this? I would have sudden thoughts and urges to scream, "I'm gay!" I looked fine to my family, but my heart was racing, and I felt like I was going to have a panic attack. My dad had always made gay jokes, and I knew he wasn't a fan of the homosexual lifestyle. This made my situation worse to the point where I was isolated and felt like I couldn't rely on anyone. I still vividly remember the times where I would try to go to sleep but would cry instead because of what was going on.

I didn't know what to do except to keep the thoughts to myself and keep checking to validate that I wasn't gay. I would try to imagine myself with a pretty girl in my class doing sexual acts to see what my groinal response would be. That was my way of handling it, and I still had no clue what was going on with me.

Then, something crazy happened.

Eventually, the thoughts stopped! I know that sounds crazy, but one day, I realized that I wasn't thinking about my sexuality anymore. I'm not sure if the reason the thoughts stopped was because of the constant reassurance I was performing, but It felt like a miracle. I still don't know why the thoughts stopped, but I was ecstatic to go back to my life before HOCD.

I must have been going into high school at this point, and I was back to thinking about normal things like video games, girls, and sports. I didn't question my sexuality anymore and stopped having unwanted sexual thoughts towards people I didn't have feelings for.

For a while, it felt like everything was back to normal. Sadly, it wasn't, and eventually, the thoughts came back.

The High School Years

Like I stated in the previous chapter, my HOCD was gone basically by the time I entered high school. I can still remember the girl I had a crush on in my PE class, and how nervous I was to be around her. I focused on being on the lacrosse team, hanging out with friends, and my HOCD seemed like a distant memory by this point.

That's how life was up until my junior year of high school. That's when everything came crashing down again.

The ironic part about this is that my HOCD came back the same way it started: through a TV show.

I had become a regular fan of this show called *Whitecollar*. The main character was Neal, played by Matt Bomer, a former con artist who helps the FBI capture other Whitecollar criminals using his own past experiences.

The show was great, and I was hooked for the first few seasons. That was until my HOCD came back and ruined my life. Matt Bomer was the lead actor, and he was one handsome fellow. I noticed that when I started watching the show, but thankfully, my OCD didn't start panicking and throwing me intrusive thoughts about kissing him. I was able to watch the show with a peaceful mind and not worry about any intrusive thoughts.

As I became more invested in the show, I started to look up the cast's history from pure curiosity. One day, I searched up Matt Bomer on Wikipedia and read a bit of his history. I was shocked at what I read.

"Matt Bomer is married to his publicist, Simon Halls."

"Wait, isn't that a guy's name?" I thought to myself. So, I looked it up, and indeed, it was a guy.

I was shocked to find out he was gay. He played a sophisticated, good looking, ladies' man on the show that I would have never guessed he could've been gay. Up until that point in my life, I always had the misconception that all gay men were feminine and talked girly. I was wrong by a long shot with this case, and it left me asking myself another what-if question. "What if I could be gay but not have feminine qualities like Matt?"

That what-if question was the only thing my brain needed to go full HOCD panic mode. From that day on, I started questioning my sexuality again based off this actor who didn't look gay but was.

I was frustrated that I was getting unwanted sexual thoughts again. The same thoughts and feelings slowly came back as well: anxiety, always questioning everything, and avoiding. "Why me!" I thought to myself. "This doesn't make any sense! I was checking out a girl's ass like last week." Those were the kind of thoughts that I would always yell out in my head. Even though I started questioning my sexuality again, I didn't use previous methods of testing myself because I always felt like what I was feeling about men wasn't real. I was still getting intrusive thoughts, but there would be days where I just knew this wasn't real.

I had the biggest crush in my sophomore year to this girl named Tanya. I thought she had the most amazing smile, and I would tense up every time I was near her. I would get nervous, try to act cool, and stay "aloof" any time she was around me. By reading that, you can probably figure out that I was terrible with women. I was legitimately scared of any girl I found attractive and didn't have the best of luck with dating in high school. Regardless, I never felt that way about a guy ever in my life and still haven't till this day.

I think having those experiences with women and having a history of being attracted to them always gave me hope that these unwanted and intrusive thoughts weren't real at all. There had to be a reason behind why I was receiving the thoughts. It turns out that there was a reason, but I didn't know it yet.

The next year and a half of high school were marred by intrusive thoughts about my sexuality while I had crushes on girls. It was ridiculous that this was happening again and I was back to square one. I found women attractive but always had that little voice saying, "But what if you're gay and you just haven't tried it yet." The thought of sexual encounters with another man was never something I wanted to do or fantasized about. This was a constant battle that never seemed to favor my side of things. It always seemed like my HOCD was getting the better of me, and I didn't know what to do. I didn't tell anyone, and I gave off the impression of everything being fine. I looked like a normal teenager, but I felt far from it.

If there was a girl who had a crush on me and I didn't find her attractive, I would start to think that it was because I might be gay. If I didn't find a certain girl attractive that others found attractive, then I would begin to assume the same thing. Everything always came back to the "what if I'm gay" question.

I remember this was the time I started questioning more things regarding sexuality and relationships. I would ask, "Imagine if being gay was considered the norm, and being straight wasn't." I kept asking questions about almost everything, and the whole purpose of life and relationships seemed like a question mark.

Logic and critical thinking were no longer a part of my life during this time, and the best thing I could do was live with it in silence.

I didn't go to any school dances in high school, except for prom. Dances weren't something that I cared about during this time, so I never really participated in that aspect of high school. Even though I didn't care about dances, some unwanted thoughts held me from going to them. I would get thoughts like "Why are you going to dances if you know that requires going with a girl? Are you going to waste her time, especially since you're gay"? I would get these thoughts regularly, and sometimes; it felt like they had a valid point. I wasn't living life to its fullest potential, and my mindset was holding back. That would perfectly sum up my high school experience.

High school wasn't the worst time, but it wasn't the greatest either. I had other issues I was dealing with like acne, shyness, social anxiety, and being insecure. That's not to say that I didn't have my share of fun moments, but it could've been better. There were times where I took relationships with girls as reassurance for HOCD instead of having fun and enjoying it.

I was only dating three girls throughout my entire time in high school. One was in my freshmen year that only lasted a week. The second one was in my junior year, and we dated for two weeks (HOCD was prevalent here). The third girl I dated was in my senior year, and that lasted for three weeks. Was I genuinely interested in any of these girls? Kind of, I wasn't into the first two girls I dated, but I did it to get my first kiss and see what it was like to be in a relationship. I was genuinely interested in the third girl I dated, but HOCD held me back in many ways. I would always get unwanted thoughts every time I would kiss her or when I was alone with her. Thoughts like "Tell her you're gay," and "Why are you wasting her time? You don't like girls" would always pop up. This would make it extremely difficult to enjoy the relationship, and I eventually broke it off with her.

Of course, other things lead me to break it off with her like her constant need for attention and the fact that I needed always to text her. However, that felt minuscule compared to dealing HOCD while being in a relationship.

The only time HOCD took a backseat was during my senior year because of all the college apps I was putting out. I was nervous that I wouldn't get into the college of my choice (I didn't), and that took up a lot of my time. Eventually, I got admission into California State University, Dominguez Hills, and was looking forward to starting a new chapter in my life.

The future looked bright at this point, and I was genuinely excited about what was to come. Unfortunately for me, my first year of college turned out to be one of the worst times for my mental health. It was during this period of my life that I knew that I couldn't live in silence anymore.

I had to be honest with myself and get some help.

The College Years

I didn't know what to expect when I went to college, and I'm still not fully able to comprehend what happened to me during this time, but I'll try my best to explain.

I still had HOCD when I started college, but I started to develop other forms of unwanted and intrusive thoughts in regards to life and existence. I still vividly remember my first day of college when I went to my 5 pm class and sat down waiting for the professor. I had my backpack, pen, notebook, and paper to take notes.

When the professor arrived, I started to take notes and listened to what he said, like everyone else was. As he started to go on about the materials, we would need, and the way the class operated, I felt a bit of panic. I started to feel anxious, and my heart was beating faster than usual. All this information about the syllabus, textbooks, and other things were all so new to me that I felt overwhelmed with the number of things we had to do.

Once the class was over, I walked to my car and kept thinking about what just happened. "Did I experience an anxiety attack, or did I just get flustered?" I didn't know what to think and on my drive home, I realized something was wrong. I felt like there was an impending danger headed towards me, and I didn't know why I felt this way. I could feel my heart beating harder and faster than usual, yet I didn't know why.

When I got home, my mom asked how my first day went, and I lied to her and told her it went well. I didn't mention the heightened anxiety and fearfulness I experienced. As I was lying about how my day went, I could feel my heart racing and feeling like that same impending doom was upon me. Again, I kept it to myself and just tried to live with it. I didn't want to worry my mom, nor did I want to confess what was truly going on with me. Sadly, it seemed like a life of lies was my only option at that point in my life.

The next few days, I started to have these weird intrusive thoughts of "Why are you going to school anyway, you should just kill yourself," or "You're no longer allowed to have fun because you're no longer in high school." I was shocked and confused as to why I was receiving these thoughts. It felt like there was someone on my shoulder telling me things that I should believe that I didn't want to.

Eventually, it got to the point where I wasn't able to see life easily, and I started questioning the meaning of life and if there was any point to it. I was becoming obsessed with finding some clarity from all of these thoughts that it drove me insane. I could go on about that, but I want to focus on the HOCD aspect.

I knew I was at a breaking point when I didn't even want to go to sleep because that meant that I was going to be alone with my thoughts and that scared the living crap out of me. I knew if I carried on like this, then I wouldn't be doing myself any favors. So, I finally told someone about it, which is something I never thought I would do.

My parents were shocked to hear what was going on and were genuinely confused about my thoughts. How could they know what was going on when I didn't even know what they were myself?

I didn't tell them about the HOCD because I was still too scared at that point to see how they would react.

Like all good parents, they wanted to know more of what was going on since they probably knew that there was more to this than I shared. It took a few days, but I ended up telling my parents about my initial homosexual thoughts when I was 12. Were they surprised? Most definitely, since I always seemed fine and never showed any possibilities that I could be gay. One of their first questions was, "So, did you figure that out yet?" I lied and said that I didn't have those thoughts anymore. I was still scared about how they would see me if I told them the truth. I knew it was wrong to lie to them, especially when I could've left everything out in the open and come clean about all of it. I knew that if I said that I was still struggling with HOCD, then my parents would start thinking that I was gay when I wasn't.

Eventually, we decided it would be better if I went to see someone professionally at my school. So, I ended up making an appointment with the school counselor. The experience didn't go too well as she didn't know how to categorize what I was dealing with, and gave me useless techniques to combat my intrusive thoughts. I remember telling her about how I was having these unwanted sexual thoughts about my sexuality, and her response was, "Oh, just tell it to shush."

"To shush?" I remember thinking at that time. "You want me just to say shush, and that'll make these thoughts from coming back?" Other techniques she offered were buying herbal remedies that "healed" unwanted thoughts and responding to me with a lot of "Oh ok, that's interesting." I probably went to 5 or 6 sessions before pulling the plug on the whole thing. She was a lovely lady nonetheless, but I still felt lost and depressed that I couldn't figure out what was wrong with me and how to tackle it.

I decided that my only option up until that point was to wait until the thoughts went away. As you can probably guess, this didn't go well for me at all. My thoughts fluctuated by the months, and it never seemed to end. Some days, I felt better and other days, I just wanted to cry and end my life.

One specific example I remember was when I was watching a movie trailer about the singer, Liberace. Youtube promoted "The trailer," and I decided to check it out by pure curiosity. While I was watching it, I could feel my heart racing and feeling a sense of panic. During this time, TV shows, and movies that contained homosexual themes were a massive trigger for my HOCD. I always had to stop watching because it felt like a panic attack was coming full force. When I felt a sense of panic coming towards me, a common method I would use would be to jump on the treadmill immediately until I'm tired. If I didn't run the thoughts off, then I would close my eyes and wait for the thoughts to stop their terror over my mind.

That was my life for many years. I would constantly use inefficient methods and deal with HOCD in silence. It always felt like there was a dark cloud following me everywhere I went, no matter what I did.

Anyone with POCD knows the struggle of wanting to give up because they feel like they will never get better. It feels like we're in an endless dark tunnel that never seems to have a light at the end of it. While we're in this tunnel, we're constantly being bombarded with excellent we don't want to have.

You might still be thinking that there's no hope while you're reading this, but I thought the same thing, and here I am writing a book on how I was able to manage them. One key moment in my life pushed me to the point of finally seeking the help I needed, and it was extraordinary.

Making the Decision to Finally Get Some Help.

One of the key things that helped me keep my OCD thoughts at ease was getting a girlfriend. Now, I know some people who suffer from HOCD steer away from getting into relationships because they start to have that thought of being in a fake relationship, or wasting the other person time if you do end up being gay. This wasn't the case for me, and in fact, it helped me exponentially.

Several months went by since my last visit with the school counselor, and as I said before, it was a bit of a roller coaster ride with my thoughts. My first year of college ended, and I had the summer to look forward to. The thoughts were still there, but it felt like they weren't as strong as they used to be. That's not to say they weren't kicking my ass every day, but not as much as before. One day, I ended up getting invited to Six Flags by some friends, and I decided to go too since I had never been and wanted to try to get over my fear of roller coasters.

While I was there, I met this girl who I instantly clicked with. The conversation felt so organic and exciting that it felt like we could talk for hours. As the day went on, we eventually stuck by each other's side the rest of the day. By the end of the day, I got her Instagram and knew there was something there. My life changed in that instance, and OCD didn't feel like a big problem anymore. I stopped thinking about the meaning of life and having these intrusive thoughts about my sexuality. Instead, I was looking at her social media every day, thinking of the right thing to text her, and trying to figure out if she was into me. I felt like a normal teenager for once, and it felt amazing.

I won't get into the details leading up to me asking her to be my girlfriend because you'd probably cringe on how bad I dealt with it, but the point was I got her to be my girlfriend after several months. This was my first real relationship, as well, and I was excited to put my HOCD finally in the past.

I was wrong.

Even though the relationship was filled with happy memories and incredible moments, my HOCD came creeping back like the virus that it was. Just when I thought I had beaten it, it came back and ruined my mental health. Now, I won't get into specific details because I don't feel comfortable putting intimate details of my past relationship out there, but some of the things that happened placed my mind in a constant panic mode. Sometimes, when she and I would be together, my mind would have the sudden urge to yell out, "I'm Gay!" Thoughts like that would freak me out because it reminded me of eating with my parents at the dinner table and having the same urge to shout that I'm gay randomly.

There would be some days where I would have a thought like, "Imagine how embarrassed she'll be if she finds out you're gay, and everyone finds out." Thoughts like that came up a lot and me being the naïve person I was, I just dealt with it by being silent. The unwanted thoughts were at their worst during the first few months of the relationship, but as time went on-- my mind was starting to have less intrusive thoughts. During the latter part of the relationship, it felt like my HOCD was transitioning to being in the trunk of the car instead of always being in the passenger seat. I would get an occasional unwanted thought, but I was too focused on being in love and had a great time with an awesome girl. Instead of having unwanted thoughts about my sexuality, I would think about Valentine's day, what I was going to plan for her birthday, and looking forward to random adventures. Don't get me wrong, I still struggled sometimes with my unwanted thoughts, but there were some days where it felt like a distant memory.

One of the reasons why I hold this relationship in such high regard until this day is because of what I was able to learn about myself, relationships, and communication. I always considered this my first real relationship because, throughout high school, most of my relationships never went past one month. This one was different, and I could sense it as time went on. I fell in love, and I learned so much from the relationship. I learned how to consider someone else's feelings, how to care for someone when they're in dire need, and I learned about the importance of sharing your feelings. Being in love is one of the most exceptional experiences a human being can have. There's joy, passion, heartbreak, and a bond that feels unbreakable. I'm truly thankful for this relationship and encourage the reader not to let HOCD control their dating life. If you feel a strong connection to someone and feel like there could be a possibility for a relationship, then go for it! Don't be afraid that you might have unwanted and intrusive thoughts during a relationship because missing out on love is an opportunity you don't want to waste. Dating, exploring places, being silly, meeting family's, going on random adventures, having someone be there for you through thick and thin is something that you should look forward to, even if you're dealing with HOCD. Trust me; it's an experience that won't ever be forgotten.

I would have never experienced one of the greatest moments of my life if I had let HOCD control my decisions. I encourage you to be the same way and experience the fantastic and depressing aspects of being in love. It will truly change you. I learned a lot about myself, and I wouldn't trade this experience for anything in the world.

The relationship was an incredible experience, but it did have its fair share of upsetting moments. It lasted a good 3 ½ years, but she ended up breaking up with me due to differences between us that were too hard to ignore anymore. This was one of the darkest times of my life. I no longer had a best friend/girlfriend that I could do stuff with. I felt alone and sad that I had lost a big part of my life.

It was during this time that my mental health worsened, and I felt like I was 18 again. I no longer had someone to go out with and keep my mind on other things, and worst of all, I had more time alone with my thoughts.

The relationship was great at helping me avoid the thoughts for a while, but I never tackled them head-on as I should have. Being with her had helped me keep my mind preoccupied with from HOCD, but it didn't tackle the root of my problem. The months following the break up really put me in a place of fear and loneliness, where I knew I needed to get help or face living a life filled with intrusive thoughts forever.

This was the first step in improving my life and a significant moment in getting serious about helping my condition.

One day, I was on Amazon looking for books to buy that could help me with my anxiety disorder, and I stumbled upon this book called, ***Overcoming Unwanted Intrusive Thoughts: A CBT-Based Guide to Getting Over Frightening, Obsessive, or Disturbing Thoughts*** by Sally Winston and Martin Seif. I saw the title, and it seemed like it would help, so I immediately ordered it. When I got the book and started reading it, I was shocked. It had every single type of OCD I could think of and had a specific way for the reader to combat their intrusive thoughts. I was amazed and wondered, "Where have you been all my life?" This was the book I needed when I was 12, and I finally had a real answer on how to identify and tackle my thoughts.

Right after I finished reading the book, I decided to tell my parents what was going on finally. I was honest about everything and told them I was planning on seeing a therapist to get the help I needed finally. It felt good, to be honest with them, but I couldn't help but notice that my dad seemed more focused on the homosexual aspect of my OCD when I told them I had multiple types. He told me that he thought I was going to end up dating men in the future, and that I would experiment with my dating life. He still calls HOCD an "emotional conflict" till this day. I chuckled at that comment because I knew my dad didn't get it and probably never will. Do I regret telling my parents? Not really. Do I think they understand my situation? Probably not since they never heard of Pure OCD before.

I had reached a point in my life where I realized that I had to be transparent and not care anymore. I kept thinking about the past ten years, where I would always lie about how I felt and how I was so sick it of it. I didn't want to live life with fear and regret anymore. The big point for me was that I was finally getting the help I needed, I was being honest, and I had a book that reassured me what I have is real and treatable.

Even though the book was a tremendous help, I still felt like going to see a therapist would be beneficial for me. The book did wonders for me in terms of showing me that I could get better and going over the exact steps to overcoming intrusive thoughts, However, I knew I had to find someone who had some experience in the OCD field, or I would run the risk of having a bad experience like with my college counselor. I had kept my thoughts hidden for so long that I knew it would be tremendously beneficial for me to share my story completely without any filter in therapy. I was prepared to cry and feel any other emotion that would come from these sessions. I didn't care thought; I just knew that I wanted to get better, and I was going to find a way to accomplish that.

I told myself, "if you don't seek the appropriate help now, then you'll never be happy." I finally had the courage after ten years of dealing with this anxiety disorder and feeling so lost throughout my life, to fully commit to improving my mental health.

What ended up happening was one of the best decisions of my life.

How I Finally Learned to Manage My Thoughts.

I had tried therapy in my second year of college but didn't commit to it. I went to one session and didn't follow through with the following appointment. My reasoning behind that? I felt that going to therapy and confronting my problems would only make my condition worse. I thought that by avoiding my thoughts, they would eventually go away. Boy, was I wrong on that? I also didn't go back because I felt like the therapist that I was speaking with didn't understand my situation. It felt like it would be a waste of time to continue the sessions with her, so I called it quits again. See where my disdain for therapists come from?

I decided to try therapy one more time but with a mindset of following through on it. I was determined to get better, and nothing was going to get in my way. I ended up getting an appointment with a therapist who specialized in OCD and intrusive thoughts.

My therapist was named Dr. Bartel, and she was a lovely woman. I consider meeting and working with her a crucial part of my improvement. Our first initial meeting was direct and to the point where we started talking about what was going on with me. I told her everything that I went through and didn't hold back. It was nerve-wracking to share with her my deepest insecurities and secrets, considering that we just met. Was it easy to do this? Not at all, it was hard to straight-up say what was bothering me.

As the sessions went on, I found myself getting more comfortable with telling her my intrusive thoughts. During our sessions, I told her about the book that I bought from Amazon and let her know how beneficial it was for my mental health. She later told me that she started reading it as well because she wanted more information on Pure OCD and how she could help future patients who dealt with the same thing. Since she was reading the book during our sessions, she was able to understand how intrusive thoughts worked, and how to incorporate some of her methods with the books to help me overcome them. Not only was I getting better, but I could feel myself going back to the mindset I had before HOCD.

I'm going to break down the three key things we went over that eventually helped me manage my thoughts.

1. **Talking about my problems.**
This was one of the things that I seriously lacked. The only people I ever told about my situation were my parents, and even then, I didn't feel like they knew what was going on, so it wasn't beneficial. All they could do was listen and offer words of support. Hearing myself say my intrusive thoughts out loud to another person made me realize how insane those thoughts were. Not only were they false, but they had no validity behind them.

It also helps when you're getting another point of view from a trained specialist because people with OCD rarely get another opinion because of the fear of judgment. I never wanted to tell anyone because I didn't want them to see me differently or treat me differently than they had before. For the first time, it felt like I could get constructive advice from someone who had expertise.

2. **Mindfulness**
   When my therapist told me about mindfulness, I had no idea what it was. "Is that something to do with thinking differently?" I asked her. What it ended up being was the state of being in the present moment, while acknowledging and accepting one's feelings, thoughts, and bodily sensations. What did this mean for me? Well, first, it meant that I had to accept my thoughts and learn to acknowledge that they are there, and there was no way I could avoid them. You can't avoid the thoughts, and if you try, it only makes your condition worse.

   This helped tremendously because I no longer tried hard to get rid of the thought by ignoring it. Instead, I acknowledged that I had it and that it was just a thought. It's easier said than done, but trust me, with practice, you will be well on your way to having a healthier mindset.

3. **The thoughts are not an accurate representation of who you are.**
   This was a big one for me and a lot of you out there. If you deal with any OCD, then you probably have crazy and unwanted thoughts that control your life. This will lead sufferers to think that their

thoughts represent who they really are and what they truly want. This mindset couldn't be further from the truth, and I'll tell you why. It turns out; many people have the kind of thoughts you have.

Some common thoughts include:
- Holding a baby and thinking about what would happen if you dropped it.
- Being near a ledge and thinking about jumping off.
- Driving a car and thinking about crashing it into oncoming traffic.
- Thoughts about killing yourself or others.
- Having intrusive sexual thoughts about friends and family members.

It is not uncommon for many ordinary people to have these kinds of unwanted thoughts. The difference between people who have those thoughts and people with Pure OCD is that people with Pure OCD are more susceptible not to let them just be thoughts. They think, "Oh my god, what does this mean?" or "But I'm not a terrible person, why would I think that?" People with OCD want to and feel like they have to figure out the meaning behind these thoughts and won't let them be random thoughts. If you're scared of your thoughts, then that is a good indicator that they do not represent who you are as a person.

4. **You're not perfect, and that's ok.**

I think as humans, we all want to do things a certain way and not mess up. Whether that's in school, relationships, or with family, we tend to be our worst critic.

Growing up, I always felt like human beings were either black or white. What I mean by that is that I thought people were either overwhelmingly good or bad. There was no in-between, and if you did something bad, then that meant you were categorized as a bad person.

I was a mess when I arrived for my first session of therapy. I was feeling hopeless on the inside, and I had hated myself for the longest time. I kept asking myself, "Why am I a bad person?" or "why do I think this way." It is a common thing to do and a habit that needs to be shut down. What I mean is that we tend to be the hardest person on ourselves. If we didn't get a specific job or things didn't work out in a particular instance, we tend to blame ourselves.

I'm sure if I asked you the last time you called yourself stupid or cursed yourself out, you'd probably give me several instances. However, can you tell me about a time where you told yourself something nice?

I remember thinking the same thing and realizing how hard I had been on myself for most of my life. I never told myself that I was proud of who I was or what I was able to accomplish. It was always negative talk that patrolled my brain.

I don't hate myself, nor should you. People make mistakes all the time, and it's up to you to be able to forgive yourself and move on. Accept that these thoughts are not an indicator of who you are, but just random thoughts that have no power.

I lasted in therapy for about four months, and I continuously got better with every visit. We started with sessions once a week, and gradually, the appointments kept getting spaced out from weeks to months. I started seeing Dr. Bartel every week, and then it was every two weeks, and before I knew it, I was able to go one whole month without seeing her. There would even be times where we would finish our sessions early, and I would share with her other aspects of my life that didn't even involve Homosexuality OCD.

As time went on, I realized that I didn't need any more sessions. I didn't have anything more to share, and I felt like I had overcome my life's most significant obstacle up until that point. I felt great mentally and was feeling excited about what the future had in store for me. So, when my next appointment arrived, I knew it would be my last. I decided to make my last session with Dr. Bartel special by writing her a letter. I wrote her a letter that described how much I appreciated her work and commitment to helping me overcome one of my biggest hurdles in life.

Once I finished reading my letter, I looked up and saw her face beaming with a joyous expression that made me smile. I could see that she was genuinely happy and proud that I was able to overcome a disorder that had plagued my life for over ten years. We exchanged a few more remarks, and I let her know that I no longer needed therapy. It felt bittersweet, but it felt like a culmination of ten years' of dealing, and finally being able to overcome intrusive and unwanted thoughts. We eventually said our goodbyes, and she let me know that if I ever needed to come back, then the opportunity would always be available. I told her that I appreciated it and that I would reach out if I needed it.

I haven't been back since.

Once I left her office for the last time, I sat in my car for a while. I felt an emotion that was too enormous to ignore. I felt a tremendous sense of triumph and happiness that I started to cry in my car. I just sat there and cried while I had the biggest smile. I wasn't crying because I was hurt or devasted, but I was crying because I never thought I would ever reach this moment. I never thought I would be able to control my Pure OCD, let alone in such a short timeframe of four months. I started having images of my twelve-year-old self crying and continually feeling like there was no hope in life anymore. The constant panicking, the constant fear of judgment, and the constant fear of living a life that felt like a lie. All that came to an end, and I was able to overcome all that. I couldn't help myself, and I continued to cry tears of happiness.

As I drove away from Dr. Bartels office, I didn't feel a sense of uncertainty or panic. The exact opposite occurred, I was excited, and most importantly, I was happy!

Do I still deal with OCD? Yes, and no. I don't deal with Homosexuality OCD anymore, but sometimes, I'll catch myself having an unwanted sexual thought from time to time. The difference is that my mental health and the way I manage my thoughts now is way better than how I managed them in the past ten years. That's where I hope the next chapter helps you figure out how to best manage your thoughts and finally get rid of that creeping anxiety that plagues you throughout your day.

What to Do When You Get an Unwanted Thought.

As you guys know, I didn't have successful methods in controlling my unwanted thoughts throughout my teen years, and into my early twenties. I made every inconceivable mistake you could imagine, and I never knew what to do when I would receive an unwanted thought. My methods involved a lot of panicking, overthinking, and "pissing the gay away." Don't worry; I'll explain what that term means.

During the early years of my encounter with HOCD, I would always feel the need to pee when I would start getting anxiety from my thoughts. According to my illogical mind, peeing would get rid of gay thoughts. It's incredible what kind of things we'll believe and do to try to stop ourselves from having these thoughts. This "peeing method" obviously didn't work at all. It only acted as reassurance, and as you all know, that doesn't solve anything. My peeing method would surprisingly, reduce my anxiety for a brief moment, but my thoughts would still be there ready for another round of panic, inducing session on my mind.

I do not want any of you reading this to go through any of that. I can vividly remember the feeling of being on the verge of a panic attack and not knowing how to stop that feeling. It is one of the worst feelings that any OCD sufferer can go through, but this chapter will show you how to minimize those thoughts and take control of your emotional state.

During the first few months of therapy, my psychologist told me about the five senses rule. I had never heard about this rule before from my previous therapists, so I was intrigued to find out how I could apply it to my life.

Dr. Bartel informed me that when I felt like I was about to be overwhelmed with anxiety, that I should use the five senses rule to be in the present moment.

The five senses rule is broken down into the following steps:

- 5 things you can touch
- 4 things you can see
- 3 things you can hear
- 2 things you can smell
- 1 thing you can taste

> The 5 senses rule has one priority, and that is to bring you back into the present moment. When you're always thinking about your thoughts, this can create a cycle of fear that causes your mind to be all over the place. When you apply the five senses rule, you're training your brain to be in the present moment, instead of being in a state of panic.
>
> This method can pull you from a state of constant worry and panic, but it takes time. It also helps to

incorporate proper breathing techniques because when we start to feel anxious, our breathing patterns are thrown off course, and it can feel like we forgot how to breathe altogether. When applying the five senses rule, remember to perform slow inhales and exhales to calm your current state. This combination can significantly reduce your thought patterns at the moment, but it will require multiple repetitions to notice significant reductions in anxiety. That is one way to deal with your intrusive thoughts, but there's also another method called the RJAFTP that was introduced by Sally Winston and Martin Seif.

RJAFTP is an acronym for Recognize, Just thoughts, Accept and allow, Float and feel, let Timepass, and Proceed[4]. I learned about this method in **Overcoming Unwanted Intrusive Thoughts,** and it has done wonders for my mental state.

Recognize

The first step is simple. You're acknowledging that you're experiencing an intrusive thought, but instead of trying to scurry the thought away, you're going to allow it to stay. You want to observe yourself while you're having these thoughts and see what kind of emotions you're feeling at the moment. You can say something like, "I have an

---

[4] Winston, Sally, and Martin N. Seif. *Overcoming Unwanted Intrusive Thoughts: a CBT-Based Guide to Getting over Frightening, Obsessive, or Disturbing Thoughts*. New Harbinger Publications, Inc., 2017.

unwanted thought right now, and it doesn't carry any importance at all."

You have to be curious and nonjudgmental as possible. Don't reason with the thought, nor should you think about what it means. Just know that it's an intrusive thought and it isn't real. When you do this, you're strengthening your ability not to be blindsided by your thoughts and to recognize that they are not dangerous at all.

Just Thoughts

Here, you'll be able to distinguish that the current thought you're having is just a random thought. It carries no weight whatsoever, and it will not affect your life in any way. During this step, I would say something like, "This is just a thought, and it carries no significant weight at all." This allowed me to see my HOCD thoughts as neutral and careless as any other thought that I thought about.

By leaving the thoughts alone, you avoid getting into a back and forth conversations with your unwanted thought, and this causes the thought to gain less importance. This step is all about reminding yourself what you already know, and that is just a random thought and nothing more.

Remember, we want you to think about HOCD like you do with any other thought. A good example is whether or not you'll enjoy eating bananas. This thought carries no significance because nothing will happen to you if you like the banana or not. You have to apply the same concept to HOCD as you would with the banana thought. They're both just random thoughts and are unimportant in your life.

Accept and Allow

This step is all about acceptance, and it might be the most challenging. You've been trying religiously to push your thoughts away at any given moment, but now, you're supposed to allow them in. Don't engage, but be an observer to what's going on. Ask questions like "What kind of thoughts am I getting?" or "I'm allowing these thoughts to roam free as I just watch from afar."

The reason why this part is one of the most complicated tasks is that HOCD sufferers always try to rationalize and make sense of every single thought. They think about what it could mean or why they are having these kinds of thoughts. **Don't do that!** It doesn't do you any good and only enhances your HOCD.

By accepting and allowing your thoughts to be in your mind, you're training your brain into categorizing your thoughts as unimportant. When your brain notices that you're allowing these thoughts to roam around instead of pushing them away, it'll begin to see that these thoughts are unimportant and harmless. This will eventually cause you to develop new habits, and you'll see your thoughts as a conversation that's not worth partaking in.

Float and Feel

Float and feel use some techniques from the five senses rule. It's all about being in the present moment and noticing what's around that you'll be seeing, hearing, and smelling. You're removing yourself from the experience of the thoughts by becoming a bystander and observing. You're allowing your thoughts to stay in your mind as much as they would like, but you'll avoid participating in any event that it's causing.

Let Time Pass

Taking your time is an essential step in healing and reprogramming yourself. There is no rush, and you should feel confident in letting your thoughts roam free. Time helps heal all wounds, and it applies to many aspects of our daily lives. How do you usually get over a bad breakup or a death in the family? It usually involves time, and we all need time to see results. Progress doesn't happen overnight, but you'll be able to see constant improvements over a significant period.

Time is your best friend here, and you have to realize that you're in no danger by having these thoughts because they're just thoughts.

Proceed

Continue practicing every step until you start feeling comfortable with your thoughts. You have to remember that you're taking away their power over you by participating in this method. Winston compares the thoughts to terrorists and how terrorists commit atrocities to change the way people live. Are you going to stop going out to clubs or bars because there was a shooting? Are you going to stop driving your car because car accidents cause numerous killings?

No! You're going to continue to live your life, and that's how it should be. Don't let your thoughts have power over you; instead, continue to live your life on your terms, and don't let these thoughts trick you into thinking that they are dangerous. They are not essential, and you will soon figure that out for yourself.

Step by Step Guide on Tackling HOCD

When I first got these kinds of thoughts, I googled things like "I have gay thoughts all of sudden even though I've always liked girls" or "I think I might be gay." What I got was a lot of forums from guys like me who were going through the same thing. They all talked about how one day they started having the "What if I'm gay" thought pop into their head and couldn't think straight anymore. During my time in reading these forums, I stumbled upon a post that mentioned "HOCD." That person said that it stands for Homosexuality OCD and that many men had it. It was a fear of thinking you might be gay when, in reality, you weren't.

I took a sigh of relief when I saw that, but it was taken quickly away when I saw others say, "HOCD is not a real thing! It's just closeted gay guys who don't want to admit that they are gays". That sparked a question in me, "what if he's right? What if we're all just in denial about our sexuality and don't want to admit that we are gay?" It was a scary thought to consider, and that made my OCD go completely crazy. Eventually, though, I realized that HOCD was an actual thing and that many people suffered from it along with having Pure OCD.

Undoubtedly, one of the best decisions you can make is to educate yourself on this topic. Not only do you need to be educated to get help, but you're also going to need it to explain to people just what it is exactly you're going through.

If you're reading this book, chances are you're at a breaking point and want to find answers, and hopefully, you'll get them here. Below is a detailed breakdown on how to conclude that HOCD is not a representation of who you are, and how to finally kick it in the ass.

1. **First, stop thinking that noticing a person of the same sex; good looking makes you gay.**
   This was a big one for me, especially after I started dealing with HOCD. I feel like men, and there is a certain stigma on how we are all supposed to act. We're all supposed to think the same, never cry, be strong, and never be emotional. Well, the truth is that men are human beings as well, and we have feelings. Instead of putting on a macho or too cool persona for people, we should try to be open about our feelings.

   During my early stages of HOCD, if I saw a guy and I noticed that he was good looking, then that would throw my mind out of sync and cause significant distress. Let's get something straight, noticing that someone of the same sex is attractive doesn't make you gay. I used to think that no straight guy would ever notice if another guy was handsome and that no guy ever thought those kinds of things. I was wrong, and it took me years to realize this.

   If you're dealing with HOCD, then any little thing can set you off. If you see a good-looking guy and you acknowledge that their pretty handsome could completely turn your mind into panic mode and make you start thinking that makes you gay. So, take a deep breath and next time you see a handsome guy, don't be afraid to admit it. After all, you're not saying you want to sleep with him.

2. **Stop avoiding certain people, places, or things.**
One of the worst things you can do is let these thoughts control what you do in your everyday life. When I first started getting my intrusive thoughts about sexuality, I couldn't watch certain TV shows, movies, or be near certain people. Avoiding certain places, objects, or people are some of the compulsions people with HOCD have, which is very counterintuitive. Exposure Response Therapy has been proven to help many OCD sufferers by repeatedly exposing them to their irrational fears.

That is exactly what you will do starting from today. You're going to stop avoiding that TV show that has tons of good-looking people in it and you're going to watch it from the beginning to the end while letting your thoughts flow through your mind. Will it be easy? God no, I'm sure you have a panic attack just reading this, but it is necessary. Any time I felt myself having an intrusive thought about a male actor on screen or anywhere, I would just let it happen again and again until it didn't matter anymore.

Overcoming anxiety will result from you constantly exposing yourself to whatever it is you're currently avoiding. When you constantly avoid, you're not training your brain to learn between actual fear and unimportant thoughts.

A great metaphor I once read described the thoughts perfectly in the sense of a playground bully. Unwanted thoughts are like a playground bully because they intimidate and scare you from doing certain things. When you go to the playground and see the bully there, you automatically want to leave or go somewhere else. You don't want to deal with the bully because you're afraid of what would happen if you stopped avoiding them.

The bully has power over you. Their presence changes the way you act and what you can do. We don't want that for you, and that's exactly how these unwanted thoughts have power over you. Once you stop watching that show or going out to certain places; you no longer have power over the thoughts. The thoughts control you, but it doesn't have to be that way.

According to Sally Winston, "In general, all avoidances reinforce and empower your unwanted intrusive thoughts. It is the exact opposite of what we want. We want your intrusions to become less powerful, and you to be less and less susceptible (Winston, 147)."

So, remember always to keep that in mind. Once you stop avoiding, you've already decided that these thoughts won't control you and how unimportant they truly they are.

3. **Talk to someone about it**
   Now, I know how hard and scary it can be to talk about these thoughts with someone. There's fear that if you tell them, then they might make fun of you, think differently of you, or tell someone else about it. I completely understand, and it's a valid point to have. You need to find someone who you think you can trust and can offer some advice on seeking help. When I first had my thoughts at 12, it scared the living crap out of me. I didn't know who to tell and what this was. I just knew that if people knew this about me, they might look at me differently.

   One of the reasons why HOCD is such a taboo subject is because people are unwilling to talk about it. When I first released my HOCD story on my YouTube channel, some people told me that they went through the same thing. It wasn't for as long as I went through it, but it surprised me that others had similar thoughts, but never spoke about them. That could be the case for you as well because one of the worst things we can do is keep our thoughts bottled inside until one day we can't take it anymore. If you don't feel comfortable going to family or friends, try joining a support group on Facebook. There are tons of online support groups that have people who freely share their stories and offer advice to anyone wanting it. Just remember that you're not alone and help is available.

4. **You have to accept your thoughts and let them just be thoughts.**
   One major flaw in the thinking of people with OCD is the way they handle their thoughts. I didn't have the correct mindset and would constantly give credibility to my unwanted thoughts for years. I see others do it in my online support groups, and they fail to see how they are not making any progress. Pure OCD sufferers tend to take a thought and give it much more weight than it needs. A great example I found was from the book, **Overcoming Unwanted Intrusive Thoughts: A CBT-Based Guide to Getting Over Frightening, Obsessive, or Disturbing Thoughts.** Dr. Winston gives a carrot example to show exactly how meaningless intrusive thoughts can be. If someone thinks, "What if I don't like carrots," then nothing is going to happen because not liking carrots won't affect them in a significant way, there is no emotional weight behind that thought because there are no consequences if they don't like carrots, and they won't obsess over it. On the other hand, if you have a thought like, "What would happen if I grab that knife and stab my leg?!"

That thought is a lot scarier because if you did that, you're potentially injuring yourself with a deep cut. So, when people tend to have the knife thought, they tend to focus and obsess over it because of the severe consequences, and they start asking themselves whether or not they want to do it, which now makes knives a trigger for that person and they avoid them at all costs. It is the same thing with HOCD, and it took me a long time to admit that. If you get a passing unwanted sexual thought about someone, you have to let it be thought and move on with your day. Once you start arguing or trying to ration with the thought, you already lost because you're giving it much more emotional weight than it deserves. So, the next time you get those kinds of thoughts, remember that they are just thoughts, and have no real meaning unless you give them any.

5. Incorporate some breathing exercises and meditation.

This doesn't seem like a big deal, but trust me, it is! We tend to forget how important our breathing can be when dealing with these kinds of intrusive thoughts. I remember how bad my anxiety would get when I was in middle school, and I would try to find some reassurance for HOCD by constantly checking and arguing with my worried voice. It would go something like this:

Worried voice: What if I'm gay now that I'm going through puberty?

False Comfort: That's insane! You've liked girls your whole life and still have crushes on girls, so why would this be true?

Worried voice: That's true, but people usually find out who they like sexually in middle school and maybe I like guys.

False Comfort: You're crazy, this isn't who you are, and you know it. Look at your dick when you sexually think of girls, you're a straight man!

As you can see, I wasn't helping myself out at all by constantly going back and forth with the thought. This would often result in some major anxiety, and I couldn't do anything but wait for my mind to calm down.

My therapist talked to me about the importance of breathing and being in the present moment, like mindfulness. Sometimes, we're so trapped in our heads that we fail to stop and breathe to calm down. If you ever find yourself in a battle between false comfort and worried voice, stop thinking and incorporate some breathing exercises or meditate. There's a great app called *Calm* that has meditating exercises for roughly 15 minutes and has helped me out when I want to be in the present moment. This goes back to step number 4, where you start your breathing exercises and get comfortable with having these kinds of thoughts, but not giving them any emotional weight.

6. **Think About Your Worst Thoughts**
   Yes, you read that right. I want you to sit down in any position you like, and I want you to think about the absolute worst thoughts that give you anxiety. You may be asking, "Do you hate me?!"

No, I don't hate you, and I'm not that mean to the point where I get pleasure from seeing others having to think of their worst thoughts purposefully. After all, most of us have spent weeks, months, and even years trying not to think about them. Guess what though? This is a crucial part of getting better, and I'll explain why.

We know that these thoughts scare and disgust you. You wouldn't be reading this book if they didn't. One of the main benefits of this method is the ability to train your brain to allow these thoughts to flow and be in your head without any disturbance. As we discussed earlier in the book, you've spent most of your life trying to find ways to avoid your thoughts, and when they did appear, you would want to get rid of them as soon as possible.

You now know that avoidance is detrimental when it comes to tackling HOCD. Avoidance validates your thoughts and makes it seem like they have power over you because you stop participating in certain activities that you previously enjoyed.

So, here's how I would lay out the process for you:

1. Find a quiet place where you can think and can't be disturbed. I recommend at least 10 to 15 minutes of practice.

2. Start by thinking of your worst thoughts, and I want you to think about the unwanted thoughts that make you feel like you're going to have an anxiety attack.

3. Allow yourself to have those thoughts and let them flow for a bit. Don't react to them, but act as a bystander and notice what's going on.

4. Once you're thinking of your most repugnant thoughts, add a bit of humor in there as well. Examples would include laughing, singing a happy song with lyrics that include your thoughts, and drawing out the thought on paper.

5. If you find yourself getting overwhelmed with your thoughts, then this would be a perfect time to introduce phrases that would help alleviate the pressure. I suggest introducing phrases like:

i) That's just a thought, and I'm allowed to have this thought.

ii) Turn what if questions into what are questions. What this means is that every time you're having those "what if" thoughts, shift your focus to your senses. Think about the present moment and what you can hear, smell, and see at that moment.

Continue to practice this method until you feel like you're getting some control over your thoughts instead of the other way around. You will feel a sense of fear and anxiousness when you begin, but as time goes by, you should continuously get better at handling your thoughts.

So, to wrap everything up, let's go over the guide

1. Don't freak out if you see a person that's good looking. It's not gay to acknowledge that someone is good looking and it happens more often than you think.
2. Stop making it worse for yourself by avoiding certain places, people, or things. I promise that this is a recipe for disaster and will only make your situation worse by giving the thought power over your everyday life.
3. Talk to a family member, friend, or someone who won't use it against you. If you can't find that person, join an online support group, or see a licensed therapist that specializes in this field.

4. Accept the fact that you have these kinds of thoughts and there's nothing wrong with that. Plenty of people have these kinds of thoughts, but it's up to you to stop it from ruining your life.
5. Breathe and meditate! Even if it's just for 15 minutes a day, this can help you in the long run and keep you from having bad anxiety attacks.
6. Think about your worst thoughts. Trust me; this works at rewiring your brain to let it know that these thoughts don't impose any danger over you.

Homework

If you guys want to get better, then you'll have to put in the work to do it. I'm glad you made the first step in buying this book to learn ways on how to help yourself. If you genuinely want to get better, you're going to have to implement some of these practices in your daily life. You have to expose yourself regularly to whatever it is that's causing these intrusive thoughts. I did it, and it was tough, but it's essential to getting better. So, that is why I have decided to give you all the homework. Exciting, I know. I'll break down the list below, and you guys can have at it in any way you prefer.

1) **Carry a picture of someone in your wallet and look at it every hour for about 5 minutes.**

The catch? The picture has to be a member of the same sex, and they have to be good-looking to the point where it makes you uncomfortable. I can already feel the anxiety from you guys on how this is going to kill you or make you go crazy. It won't be the end of the world, trust me. The point of these exercises is to desensitize you to what makes you anxious. So, I suggest carrying a picture that is provocative as well. So, shirtless picks for guys and lingerie pictures for women. This might be hard at first, but it's something I recommend trying. Trust me, over time, a lot of these challenges won't feel like challenges at all.

2) **Watch a show that has gay people, or a show that involves a storyline around a person who struggled with their sexuality**.
   I remember when I first got my thoughts, I was scared as hell to watch anything that involved gay people. There was a show called *Degrassi* that I was able to watch before I developed HOCD but had to stop because the show dealt with many teenager themes like coming out, bullying, and abuse. If there were a scene that involved a character struggling with their sexuality, I would immediately start getting anxious by comparing my thoughts to their struggle. Being able to watch movies or shows that involve gay people or themes is a crucial step in progressing because most guys that struggle with HOCD tend to stop watching anything that has gay themes in it. They start to

ask themselves if they have exhibited any similar qualities to the struggle of the gay person on the show or start to think that they will experience similar situations.

3) Watch a show with a lot of good-looking people in it.

When I was 14, I enjoyed watching this show called Teen-Wolf. It was on MTV, and I enjoyed it for the storyline and just thought it was interesting. A lot of people, on the other hand, especially women, watched the show for the male characters. "Oh my God, he's so cute. Did you see last night's episode where he took his shirt off?" That wasn't me at all.

Sure, the show had tons of attractive looking young men for the female audience, but I could care less. My HOCD managed to dwindle for a bit at this point, but when It came back, I stopped watching the show. Why? Because the show had many good-looking guys on it, and I started focusing on that aspect only when my HOCD came back. I could no longer focus on the story or anything that I cared about. It was always about the fear of finding some of those guys attractive, and I didn't want to deal with that.

Don't make that same mistake and I wish I didn't. I didn't have anyone helping me, nor did I know what I was going through. Continue to watch those shows and get uncomfortable. It's necessary, and it is something that I did as well, which did help.

4) Tell someone you trust

I recommend telling your significant other if you have one, or someone you feel like you can trust. A lot of us feel alone in our everyday struggles by thinking that no one will understand what we're going through. The truth is, you might be surprised at how many people have similar thoughts but don't talk about them. When I released my Pure OCD story to my Youtube channel, I had some friends message me telling me that they went through something similar. They questioned their sexuality or would have a recurring uncomfortable thought about kissing a friend.

I was shocked that some people went through something similar because I always felt like no one would ever have a condition similar to mine. Sure, their struggles weren't as extreme, but it was comforting to hear other people's stories. Remember, if you feel like you can trust them, let them know, and maybe they can help in some way.

5) Stop watching porn

Like I discussed earlier in the book, many sufferers tend to look at porn to reassure themselves that they are not gay. Usually, this will involve the sufferer to watch all types of porn and see if they have a stimulating response in the groin area. I've already discussed why this technique is useless and why it does more harm than good. Constant reassurance only leads to more questions and doubts. It can make you feel better for a moment, but before you know it, you're back at it again questioning yourself. For a lot of men, porn can be a severe addiction, and they can't go a day without it. That addiction can grow when you're in constant fear of being something that you're not and need reassurance because you're scared.

Many men who watch gay porn might get groinal responses because of the sexual nature of the video alone. They're not attracted to men, but sexual acts, in general, can stimulate anyone under the right circumstances. If you see men kissing each other or dry humping, the acts alone can cause you to have stimulating feelings even though you don't necessarily find the men attractive. So, for now, give up the porn and if you need to release sexual tension, masturbate once a week.

6) Expose, and don't overthink

This will be the hardest thing you have to do. You might start getting an anxiety attack just by reading this. When you're looking at that picture from your wallet or watching a show that makes you feel uncomfortable because of the attractive cast members. Remember, it is just a thought. You have to remember that because that is key when you're exposing yourself.

When you get a groinal response, or you feel like you're getting the urge to do something sexual, you have to remember that you're experiencing thought-action fusion. Remember that they are just thoughts and have no power unless you give them power. Once you start getting scared by the thought or try finding every single answer about your sexuality, you've already lost.

Expose yourself to EVERYTHING that scares you and watch how you slowly stop caring for a specific time. A perfect example is a roller coaster, and I'll tell you why.

Let's think about it this way.
1. When the roller coaster is slowly ascending to the top, this is where you feel anxious (this represents the initial exposure).
2. Then there's the high point of the roller coaster. You're at the top, and you see how high you are. You realize you're about to fall and your stomach is about to turn upside down. This represents the intrusive thoughts kicking in and the feeling of no going back. They're here, and you have to deal with them.
3. The dreaded fall and depending on the person, the worst or best part of the roller coaster. For this comparison, we'll assume we all hate the drop. The drop represents getting hit with all the intrusive thoughts you hate. "What if I'm gay" "He/she is cute" or "I have a groinal response."
It's all coming down on you, and you have to deal with the rush and unexpected twist of events.
4. After we have a fall, we have the most enjoyable part of the roller coaster, at least, for me it is. The loops and turns that make us cheer and shout with excitement, but also throw us off and can give us surprises.

This is the part that will be the easiest for you. Once you had the drop and you got past the initial scare, you find yourself feeling like you're going to be ok. Yeah sure, you're going to have your unexpected turns and low points, but that's part of getting better. Behind every success, multiple failures preceded it.

So, when you're on the roller coaster, and you feel every single sensation you can think of, remember to brace yourself but enjoy the roller coaster and all of its unexpected twists as well.

Embrace Your Sexuality

You might be wondering what's embracing your sexuality means. It could be the first time you've ever been told to do this, but I'll explain why it is crucial.

I recently read a book called **NO MORE MR. NICE GUY**, by Robert A. Glover. The book talks about how many men grow up to be too nice to the point where it's ruining their marriages and holding them back in life, sex, and career. One of the key things that stood out to me was when Glover stated that "Nice Guys" believe they are bad for being sexual.

What exactly does this mean? It means that most nice guys tend to have hidden sexual behaviors because they grew up to believe that wanting to be sexual made them feel like perverts or bad people.

Does this sound familiar to any of you? I couldn't believe what I had just read when I saw that because that was exactly how I felt growing up. There would be times when I would check out a girl, and of course, I would stare at her curves and butt. The problem was that I had this little voice in my head that would tell me that it was bad to see girls that way. You had to respect them and not see them as objects. So, if I ever found myself checking out a girl, I felt ashamed of it.

I felt this sense of shame in regards to sexual attraction towards women for many reasons. I never really agreed with how certain men talked about women; this included some guys I was friends with. Referring to them as bitches or just talking about their physical traits constantly like nothing else mattered. It felt like I was being a pig and demeaning them.

There were other times where I felt like I was being shamed for showing an attraction to women. I could remember this one time in high school, my friend and I were waiting in the lunch line, and we saw this gorgeous girl walk past us. Our initial reaction was to look at and examine her from top to bottom. Another friend, who was a girl, saw how we were reacting and called us pigs for checking her out. I laughed and brushed it off like her comment meant nothing to me, but it did leave me wondering. Is it bad to check out girls in a sexual manner?

This mentality stuck with me for many years. I felt a sense of shame for being a guy and having sexual urges. When I was with friends, and everyone was talking about girls, I would stay quiet because I didn't want to seem like "another pig." This mindset, however, wouldn't stop me from masturbating in private and releasing my inner sexual desires.

All of this confused me even more, especially when I was trying to figure out if I was gay or not. I found girls sexually attractive but felt bad for checking them out. Also, I felt like there could be a possibility that I was gay, and this mindset felt like it reassured that the HOCD could be more real than I thought.

So, why is this important? First, if you're already dealing with HOCD and you have this backward mentality on being a normal sexual man, then it could be detrimental to your well-being. When I was suffering through this stage in my life, there was a constant battle in my head over whether or not my attitudes towards women had anything to do with my sexuality.

Some common thoughts would consist of:

"Why do I feel guilty about checking that girl out? Is this a sign I don't want to check her out at all?"

"Would a straight guy feel this way?"

As you can imagine, this didn't do my HOCD any favors. It took me years to finally realize that craving sex and checking out girls is human nature. I had heard women say some of the most shocking sexual things when they were describing men they found attractive. Let's say they weren't exactly talking about running through a field of roses.

Sex feels good, and it shouldn't be looked at as disgusting. Sex is a natural human need, and you shouldn't feel like a terrible person for wanting it. If you do, you'll never be able to fully express your emotions sexually with your partner, and you might not ever be ok with your sexual pleasure.

If you're dealing with HOCD and you have a partner that you're currently sleeping with, then this is vital to you.

How many times do sufferers have sex with their partner, only to think about things they don't want to think about. They can't enjoy the moment and the intimacy that sex can bring them. A lot of times, people will want to stop practicing sex all together with their partners because they want to avoid having unwanted thoughts.

Is this a good idea? Hell no! You don't want to take away an essential part of any relationship and run the risk of making it seem like your partner is the reason you can't perform. This can lead to some severe problems in your relationship and eventually, cause a breakup.

So, what should you do?

1. Don't feel ashamed of being sexually attracted to the opposite sex. It's perfectly natural, and everyone does it.
2. Don't stop having sex. Many psychologists recommend that people continue with sex because they don't want their intrusive thoughts to have any control over them. Continue to perform sexual acts and if you get a thought, try to get amused by it instead of letting it throw you off.
3. Let yourself masturbate freely and accept that you can give yourself sexual pleasure.
4. Check out all the women you find attractive and don't feel bad for doing it! You're a human being with needs, and it is perfectly normal to feel sexual desires.

Let's recap
- Don't think that you're a bad person for wanting sex, or having sexual desires.
    o Continue performing sexual acts even if you're having unwanted thoughts.
- Practice healthy masturbation and be ok with pleasuring yourself.
- Don't let your HOCD control your sexuality.

Current Outlook on OCD

I don't only suffer from Homosexuality OCD, but I wanted to mainly focus on that aspect because sexuality is a very taboo subject. Having fears of being something that you're not can be horrifying and lead you to the point of suicide. There are still some people out there who don't believe HOCD is a real thing; in fact, they think it's homophobic as they believe you're terrified of being gay. This couldn't be further from the truth, and many people might not know that gay people also suffer from this form of OCD where they fear that they might be attracted to the person of the opposite sex. Crazy, I know.

When I started going to therapy, I realized how my mindset was one of my biggest obstacles to overcome. The way I thought about OCD and how people would perceive it held back my growth and improvement for so many years. Going to therapy made me realize that a lot of the "weird" thoughts I get are very common among the general public. No one ever talks about it, so it's discussed rarely, which is counterintuitive to what we should be doing.

Sometimes, I'll people-watch from time to time and think about how many people walking across from me have their mental issues. Whether its anxiety, depression, bipolar disorder, or anorexia, people deal with personal issues all the time. I know from experience that you can't judge a person's life based off of face value. Humans are complex beings, and they have so many emotions that it can be tough to see what's going on in their lives truly.

I'm no longer afraid to talk about HOCD with anyone; in fact, I make full-fledged videos on YouTube about my experiences and offer advice. My mindset from when I was 12 to now as a 23-year-old is a drastic improvement. I'm no longer afraid of being judged, treated differently, or having those discussions because I know who I am. For so long, I thought that these thoughts represented some hidden urge to do all the things that my unwanted thoughts wanted me to do. I know now that that is no longer the case, and I want to help other people who are going through the same thing.

I want a young boy or a girl to find this book because I know how tough it can be to live with this for years without getting help because of shame and guilt. Many people don't know what they have or how to deal with, and it saddens me. Every single day, I see on my online support group, people who feel defeated all the time. People who suffer from HOCD, POCD, Harm OCD, and many other types that would make any person go insane. I see constant posts like, "Do these thoughts make me a bad person," or "I feel so guilty that I have these thoughts that I want to die?"

Those people are still in a dark stage in their life and need to keep fighting because there can be a way to manage these thoughts. Can you be cured? That's a tough question to answer because what is considered cured? Is someone ever cured of their anxiety, depression, or insomnia? Probably not, but we can find ways to help ourselves get better and live a happy life while managing these thoughts.

I have found that HOCD is something that many men and women deal with, but never admit it to the people they care about. Why? It usually comes down to shame and worry. Many people who have gone through HOCD share with me that they could never tell anyone because of the amount of shame it would bring upon them or their family. They fear distant family members gossiping about them if they were ever to find out. My response to that is usually "Who cares?" Why do other people's opinions matter when you know who you are, and what you stand for? You know what is factual about yourself, not other people.

I remember my dad came into my room a few days after I uploaded my Pure OCD video on Youtube. He told me that he was surprised that I would talk about my issues in public so freely, and he advised me that it could be detrimental to my name. He thought that if family members saw my video, then they would think differently of me and word would get around that I was confused about my sexuality. He advised me that it would be a better idea if I didn't put out videos where I discussed my personal life to avoid rumors about me being spread. What was my response to all that? I said, "I don't give a shit what people think of me. I know who I am and what I stand for. If people want to talk about it, then that's their right, but I'm not going to let people's opinions of me interfere with my goal of making a difference in people's lives."

I wish others had the same mindset of not caring what people thought of them. However, I understand that for many people, discussing HOCD in public would not be something that they would want to do. Some people grow up in religious households, and others have a public persona that they would like to keep for people to see. Sadly, many people would rather go that route instead of being transparent about their condition.

I understand that it can be difficult to completely be open about something that you've been lying about for so many years. People were legitimately surprised when I uploaded my video about my intrusive thoughts. I got messages from people telling me that they thought it was a brave thing to do, and they would have never guessed that I was suffering mentally.

I get messages from people all the time through email, social media, and Youtube about how my videos made them feel better about their HOCD situation. They still deal with unwanted thoughts, but it's comforting for them to know that there are others just like them. I've helped people privately and publicly, and that brings me so much joy. Hearing people tell me that I'm making a difference in their lives, and how much they appreciate me giving my time to help them out is what I've wanted since I started my channel.

That is the ultimate goal: to share knowledge and spread awareness that HOCD is real and needs to be taken seriously. If I'm one of those people breaking the stigma about OCD, then I'll happily take the job and share my knowledge with as many people as I possibly can. I'm already doing that, and I can't wait to reach more people and help them with their journey.

I know I'm not "cured," but my mental health is better now than it ever has been. That is something to be proud of. That is why if I can do it, so can you. Don't let these thoughts control your mind and your life. You can get better, but you're going to have to put in the work to get to where you want to be. It may take weeks, months, or even years, but you have to give it your full effort to beat this and be the person you know you are.

What to do if this book wasn't enough?

Well, I'm pretty disappointed that this book couldn't help you find ways to manage your thoughts. I know it's not your fault and I would never blame you. Having HOCD is a horrible thing, and it will take quite a while to heal and get better.

If you still find yourself being bombarded with unwanted and intrusive thoughts about your sexuality, then I recommend seeing a therapist. As much as I have trashed certain therapists in this book, not all of them are useless.

I was lucky enough to get paired with a therapist who understood what was going on with me. She had a general idea of what POCD was, and had a list of things that helped with anxiety and other mental issues. Going through this alone can be pretty hard, but having someone by your side can be very beneficial.

Several therapists who don't quite understand what POCD is and how to implement exposure prevention therapy. I've lived through that experience, and it can be demoralizing to have a licensed professional give you counteractive advice. Usually, the best-equipped therapists to handle people with HOCD are ones that have practiced exposure and response therapy (ERP), and acceptance and commitment therapy (ACP).

If you guys don't know where to start, here is a list of websites that help you look up therapists who specialize in POCD and subsets of it.

- Psychology Today Directory
- IOCDF Directory
- OCD Action
- OCD Referral/Resource Consulting
- The Center for Cognitive-Behavioral Psychotherapy
- The OCD and Anxiety Center of Greater Baltimore
- OCD Center of Los Angeles: The Anxiety Treatment Center of Greater Chicago

The best website to go to is intrusivethoughts.org. This was the first website that opened my eyes to the complex world of POCD. Everything on the site went in detail on what HOCD is, how to control it, and ways you can get involved. It goes over every type of OCD and gives excellent advice on how to seek treatment. The person behind the site also suffers from POCD and has done numerous interviews with licensed psychologists that discuss HOCD and other types of OCD.

Recap

So, lets recap and start from the beginning.

1. The thoughts do not represent who you are as a person.
2. Learn to accept the thoughts and let them flow without judgment.

3. Practice Mindfulness.
4. Embrace Your Sexuality.
5. Join a support group on Facebook.
6. See a professional.
7. Tell yourself that it is going to be ok and that these thoughts are just ...wait for it... thoughts.

Can You Do Me A Favor?
Thank you for buying and reading my book. I'm confident that you're well on your way to making significant progress in managing your HOCD knowledge if you follow the steps I've laid out here.

Before you go, I have a small favor to ask. Would you take a minute to write a brief review about this book on Amazon? Reviews are the best way for independent authors (like me) to get noticed and sell more books. I also read every review and use the feedback to write future revisions – and future books, even.

About the author
Osvaldo Jimenez is a college graduate with a B.A. in Business Administration, Youtuber, and striving entrepreneur. You can find more of his content on his YouTube channel called Ozzy Jimenez.

Bibliography

Intrusive Thoughts. "OCD Therapy (ERP, CBT, ACT)." *Intrusive Thoughts*, www.intrusivethoughts.org/ocd-treatment/ocd-therapy/

"How Do I Know I'm Not Really Gay?" *International OCD Foundation*, iocdf.org/expert-opinions/homosexual-obsessions/.

Winston, Sally, and Martin N. Seif. *Overcoming Unwanted Intrusive Thoughts: a CBT-Based Guide to Getting over Frightening, Obsessive, or Disturbing Thoughts*. New Harbinger Publications, Inc., 2017.

Intrusive Thoughts. "Pure OCD." *Intrusive Thoughts*, www.intrusivethoughts.org/ocd-symptoms/pure-ocd/.

McGowan, Kat. "Mind Control: Unwanted Thoughts." *Psychologytoday.com*, 2004, www.psychologytoday.com/us/articles/200401/mind-control-unwanted-thoughts.

"Sexual Orientation OCD Part 4: OCD & Anxiety Center of Baltimore." *OCD & Anxiety Center of Baltimore | Jon Hershfield, MFT*, 17 May 2019, www.ocdbaltimore.com/hocd-sexual-orientation-ocd-denial/.

"Obsessive-Compulsive Disorder (OCD)." *HelpGuide.org*, 30 July 2019, www.helpguide.org/articles/anxiety/obssessive-compulsive-disorder-ocd.htm.

Printed in Great Britain
by Amazon